# A First-Start® Easy Reader

This easy reader contains only 58 different words, repeated often to help the young reader develop word recognition and interest in reading.

| | | | |
|---|---|---|---|
| a | fun | Mom | stars |
| about | games | Mrs. | stories |
| and | good | music | tale |
| arrive | he | Nat | the |
| asleep | her | Nibble | then |
| baby-sitter | his | no | things |
| but | how | not | time |
| Dad | I | oh | to |
| different | in | once | TV |
| dinner | is | own | upon |
| does | it | pancakes | want |
| doing | like | play | watch |
| fairy | likes | plays | way |
| falls | make | says | |
| for | makes | she | |

# Oh, No! A Baby-Sitter!

by Justine Korman Fontes
illustrated by Dana Regan

Copyright © 2001 by Troll Communications L.L.C.

FIRST START is a registered trademark of Troll Communications L.L.C.

All rights reserved. No part of this book may be reproduced or utilized in any form or by any means, electronic or mechanical, including photocopying, recording, or by any information storage and retrieval system, without written permission from the publisher.

Printed in Canada.                ISBN 0-8167-7227-4

10 9 8 7 6 5 4 3 2

Nat does not want a baby-sitter!
A baby-sitter is not Mom.
A baby-sitter is not Dad.

Mrs. Nibble is different.
She does things her own way.

Mrs. Nibble says, "How about pancakes?"
Nat says, "Mom does not make pancakes for dinner."

Mrs. Nibble says, "I make pancakes for dinner."
She makes pancakes her way!

Her way is different.
But dinner is good!

Then Nat says, "I play games."
But Mrs. Nibble does not play
the way Nat plays.

# Mrs. Nibble plays her own way.

It is fun!

Then Nat says, "I like to watch TV."
But Mrs. Nibble does not watch TV.
She likes stories.

She says, "Once upon a time . . ."

. . . and Nat is in a fairy tale!

Mrs. Nibble does not play music the way Dad does.

Mrs. Nibble plays music her own way.
It is fun!

Nat and Mrs. Nibble watch the stars.

Nat falls asleep.

# Mom and Dad arrive.

Nat says, "Mrs. Nibble is different. She does things her own way!"

"Mrs. Nibble plays music her own way."
Nat makes music!

Nat likes doing things his own way.
And he likes his baby-sitter!